Embrace ALL that is YOU

Listen MORE to your ♡

& LESS to your mind

It's ok to let go of People things feelings

BE GRATEFUL For where you at

&

BE EXCITED About where you are going

<u>Love note:</u>
If you have enjoyed this book, it
would mean the world to me if
you could leave an honest review
on amazon and help me create
more fun books
like this one!

January 1

What is your number one goal this year?

Year _____

_____
_____
_____
_____

Year _____

_____
_____
_____
_____

Year _____

_____
_____
_____
_____

Year _____

_____
_____
_____
_____

Year _____

_____
_____
_____
_____

January 2

What is your best memory of last year?

Year _____

_____
_____
_____
_____

Year _____

_____
_____
_____
_____

Year _____

_____
_____
_____
_____

Year _____

_____
_____
_____
_____

Year _____

_____
_____
_____
_____

January 3

What made you smile today?

Year _____

_____
_____
_____
_____

Year _____

_____
_____
_____
_____

Year _____

_____
_____
_____
_____

Year _____

_____
_____
_____
_____

Year _____

_____
_____
_____
_____

January 4

What made you upset today?

Year _____

_____
_____
_____
_____

Year _____

_____
_____
_____
_____

Year _____

_____
_____
_____
_____

Year _____

_____
_____
_____
_____

Year _____

_____
_____
_____
_____

January 5

What was the last new thing you tried?

Year _____

_____
_____
_____
_____

Year _____

_____
_____
_____
_____

Year _____

_____
_____
_____
_____

Year _____

_____
_____
_____
_____

Year _____

_____
_____
_____
_____

January 6

What mood were you in today?

Year _____

_____
_____
_____
_____

Year _____

_____
_____
_____
_____

Year _____

_____
_____
_____
_____

Year _____

_____
_____
_____
_____

Year _____

_____
_____
_____
_____

January 7

What is your super power?

Year _____

_____
_____
_____
_____

Year _____

_____
_____
_____
_____

Year _____

_____
_____
_____
_____

Year _____

_____
_____
_____
_____

Year _____

_____
_____
_____
_____

January 8

What did you learn today?

Year _____

_____
_____
_____
_____

Year _____

_____
_____
_____
_____

Year _____

_____
_____
_____
_____

Year _____

_____
_____
_____
_____

Year _____

_____
_____
_____
_____

January 9

How do you feel right this moment?

Year _____

_____
_____
_____
_____

Year _____

_____
_____
_____
_____

Year _____

_____
_____
_____
_____

Year _____

_____
_____
_____
_____

Year _____

_____
_____
_____
_____

January 10

What is a fear you'd like to get over?

Year _____

_____
_____
_____
_____

Year _____

_____
_____
_____
_____

Year _____

_____
_____
_____
_____

Year _____

_____
_____
_____
_____

Year _____

_____
_____
_____
_____

January 11

What makes you smile?

Year _____

_____
_____
_____
_____

Year _____

_____
_____
_____
_____

Year _____

_____
_____
_____
_____

Year _____

_____
_____
_____
_____

Year _____

_____
_____
_____
_____

January 12

List 5 things you love about yourself.

Year _____

_____
_____
_____
_____

Year _____

_____
_____
_____
_____

Year _____

_____
_____
_____
_____

Year _____

_____
_____
_____
_____

Year _____

_____
_____
_____
_____

January 13

List 5 priorities of yours.

Year _____

_____
_____
_____
_____

Year _____

_____
_____
_____
_____

Year _____

_____
_____
_____
_____

Year _____

_____
_____
_____
_____

Year _____

_____
_____
_____
_____

January 14

Who are the people in this world you love the most?

Year _____

_____
_____
_____
_____

Year _____

_____
_____
_____
_____

Year _____

_____
_____
_____
_____

Year _____

_____
_____
_____
_____

Year _____

_____
_____
_____

January 15

Who or what inspires you?

Year _____

_____
_____
_____
_____

Year _____

_____
_____
_____
_____

Year _____

_____
_____
_____
_____

Year _____

_____
_____
_____
_____

Year _____

_____
_____
_____
_____

January 16

What is one word that describes your day?

Year _____

_____

_____

_____

_____

Year _____

_____

_____

_____

_____

Year _____

_____

_____

_____

_____

Year _____

_____

_____

_____

_____

Year _____

_____

_____

_____

_____

January 17

What is one thing you'd like to do more?

Year _____

_____
_____
_____
_____

Year _____

_____
_____
_____
_____

Year _____

_____
_____
_____
_____

Year _____

_____
_____
_____
_____

Year _____

_____
_____
_____
_____

January 18

What is your biggest fear?

Year _____

_____
_____
_____
_____

Year _____

_____
_____
_____
_____

Year _____

_____
_____
_____
_____

Year _____

_____
_____
_____
_____

Year _____

_____
_____
_____
_____

January 19

One thing you need to let go?

Year _____

_____
_____
_____
_____

Year _____

_____
_____
_____
_____

Year _____

_____
_____
_____
_____

Year _____

_____
_____
_____
_____

Year _____

_____
_____
_____
_____

January 20

What makes you proud of yourself?

Year _____

_____
_____
_____
_____

Year _____

_____
_____
_____
_____

Year _____

_____
_____
_____
_____

Year _____

_____
_____
_____
_____

Year _____

_____
_____
_____
_____

January 21

What is something funny that happened to you recently?

Year _____

_____
_____
_____
_____

Year _____

_____
_____
_____
_____

Year _____

_____
_____
_____
_____

Year _____

_____
_____
_____
_____

Year _____

_____
_____
_____
_____

January 22

Who do you miss the most in your life?

Year _____

_____
_____
_____
_____

Year _____

_____
_____
_____
_____

Year _____

_____
_____
_____
_____

Year _____

_____
_____
_____
_____

Year _____

_____
_____
_____
_____

January 23

What's your favorite movie of all time?

Year _____

_____
_____
_____
_____

Year _____

_____
_____
_____
_____

Year _____

_____
_____
_____
_____

Year _____

_____
_____
_____
_____

Year _____

_____
_____
_____
_____

January 24

What's your Affirmation for today?

Year _____

_____
_____
_____
_____

Year _____

_____
_____
_____
_____

Year _____

_____
_____
_____
_____

Year _____

_____
_____
_____
_____

Year _____

_____
_____
_____

January 25

What would you like to change in your routine?

Year _____

_____
_____
_____
_____

Year _____

_____
_____
_____
_____

Year _____

_____
_____
_____
_____

Year _____

_____
_____
_____
_____

Year _____

_____
_____
_____
_____

January 26

What is your biggest regret?

Year _____
_____
_____
_____
_____

Year _____
_____
_____
_____
_____

Year _____
_____
_____
_____
_____

Year _____
_____
_____
_____
_____

Year _____
_____
_____
_____
_____

January 27

What would you like to learn if
you had the chance?

Year _____

_____
_____
_____
_____

Year _____

_____
_____
_____
_____

Year _____

_____
_____
_____
_____

Year _____

_____
_____
_____
_____

Year _____

_____
_____
_____
_____

January 28

What's your main source of distraction?

Year _____

_____
_____
_____
_____

Year _____

_____
_____
_____
_____

Year _____

_____
_____
_____
_____

Year _____

_____
_____
_____
_____

Year _____

_____
_____
_____
_____

January 29

How hard/easy is it for you to
express your feelings?

Year _____

_____
_____
_____
_____

Year _____

_____
_____
_____
_____

Year _____

_____
_____
_____
_____

Year _____

_____
_____
_____
_____

Year _____

_____
_____
_____
_____

January 30

What is your favorite quote?

Year _____

_____
_____
_____
_____

Year _____

_____
_____
_____
_____

Year _____

_____
_____
_____
_____

Year _____

_____
_____
_____
_____

Year _____

_____
_____
_____
_____

January 31

How does your ideal day look?

Year _____
_____
_____
_____
_____

Year _____
_____
_____
_____
_____

Year _____
_____
_____
_____
_____

Year _____
_____
_____
_____
_____

Year _____
_____
_____
_____
_____

February 1

What do you feel like doing today?

Year _____

_____
_____
_____
_____

Year _____

_____
_____
_____
_____

Year _____

_____
_____
_____
_____

Year _____

_____
_____
_____
_____

Year _____

_____
_____
_____
_____

February 2

How would
your parents describe you?

Year _____

_____
_____
_____
_____

Year _____

_____
_____
_____
_____

Year _____

_____
_____
_____
_____

Year _____

_____
_____
_____
_____

Year _____

_____
_____
_____
_____

February 3

How would
your friends describe you?

Year _____

_____
_____
_____
_____

Year _____

_____
_____
_____
_____

Year _____

_____
_____
_____
_____

Year _____

_____
_____
_____
_____

Year _____

_____
_____
_____
_____

February 4

How would
you describe yourself?

Year _____

_____
_____
_____
_____

Year _____

_____
_____
_____
_____

Year _____

_____
_____
_____
_____

Year _____

_____
_____
_____
_____

Year _____

_____
_____
_____
_____

February 5

Does it matter, what other people think of you?

Year _____

_____
_____
_____
_____

Year _____

_____
_____
_____
_____

Year _____

_____
_____
_____
_____

Year _____

_____
_____
_____
_____

Year _____

_____
_____
_____
_____

February 6

If you had more free time, how would you spend it?

Year _____

_____
_____
_____
_____

Year _____

_____
_____
_____
_____

Year _____

_____
_____
_____
_____

Year _____

_____
_____
_____
_____

Year _____

_____
_____
_____
_____

February 7

What new
skills do you want to learn?

Year _____

_____
_____
_____
_____

Year _____

_____
_____
_____
_____

Year _____

_____
_____
_____
_____

Year _____

_____
_____
_____
_____

Year _____

_____
_____
_____
_____

February 8

What was your childhood dream job?

Year _____

_____
_____
_____
_____

Year _____

_____
_____
_____
_____

Year _____

_____
_____
_____
_____

Year _____

_____
_____
_____
_____

Year _____

_____
_____
_____
_____

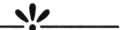

February 9

How satisfied are you with your
life right now?

Year _____

_____
_____
_____
_____

Year _____

_____
_____
_____
_____

Year _____

_____
_____
_____
_____

Year _____

_____
_____
_____
_____

Year _____

_____
_____
_____
_____

February 10

Does your work make you feel happy?

Year _____

_____
_____
_____
_____

Year _____

_____
_____
_____
_____

Year _____

_____
_____
_____
_____

Year _____

_____
_____
_____
_____

Year _____

_____
_____
_____
_____

February 11

If you didn't have to work for money,
what would you do?

Year _____

_____
_____
_____
_____

Year _____

_____
_____
_____
_____

Year _____

_____
_____
_____
_____

Year _____

_____
_____
_____
_____

Year _____

_____
_____
_____
_____

February 12

What is one thing you wish someone would have told you when you were younger?

Year _____

_____
_____
_____
_____

Year _____

_____
_____
_____
_____

Year _____

_____
_____
_____
_____

Year _____

_____
_____
_____
_____

Year _____

_____
_____
_____
_____

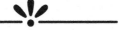

February 13

What's your
favorite thing about yourself?

Year _____

_____
_____
_____
_____

Year _____

_____
_____
_____
_____

Year _____

_____
_____
_____
_____

Year _____

_____
_____
_____
_____

Year _____

_____
_____
_____
_____

February 14

What would you want to change about yourself?

Year _____

_____
_____
_____
_____

Year _____

_____
_____
_____
_____

Year _____

_____
_____
_____
_____

Year _____

_____
_____
_____
_____

Year _____

_____
_____
_____
_____

February 15

What makes you feel alive?

Year _____

_____
_____
_____
_____

Year _____

_____
_____
_____
_____

Year _____

_____
_____
_____
_____

Year _____

_____
_____
_____
_____

Year _____

_____
_____
_____
_____

February 16

Where do you see yourself in 5 years?

Year _____
_____
_____
_____
_____

Year _____
_____
_____
_____
_____

Year _____
_____
_____
_____
_____

Year _____
_____
_____
_____
_____

Year _____
_____
_____
_____
_____

February 17

What did you have for lunch today?

Year _____

_____
_____
_____
_____

Year _____

_____
_____
_____
_____

Year _____

_____
_____
_____
_____

Year _____

_____
_____
_____
_____

Year _____

_____
_____
_____
_____

February 18

If you were granted three wishes, what would you wish for?

Year _____

_____
_____
_____
_____

Year _____

_____
_____
_____
_____

Year _____

_____
_____
_____
_____

Year _____

_____
_____
_____
_____

Year _____

_____
_____
_____
_____

February 19

What possession could you not live without?

Year _____

_____
_____
_____
_____

Year _____

_____
_____
_____
_____

Year _____

_____
_____
_____
_____

Year _____

_____
_____
_____
_____

Year _____

_____
_____
_____
_____

February 20

What was the last major
accomplishment you had?

Year _____

_____
_____
_____
_____

Year _____

_____
_____
_____
_____

Year _____

_____
_____
_____
_____

Year _____

_____
_____
_____
_____

Year _____

_____
_____
_____
_____

February 21

What did you get done today?

Year _____

_____
_____
_____
_____

Year _____

_____
_____
_____
_____

Year _____

_____
_____
_____
_____

Year _____

_____
_____
_____
_____

Year _____

_____
_____
_____
_____

February 22

What made today unusual?

Year _____

_____
_____
_____
_____

Year _____

_____
_____
_____
_____

Year _____

_____
_____
_____
_____

Year _____

_____
_____
_____
_____

Year _____

_____
_____
_____

February 23

What was your last major purchase?

Year _____

_____
_____
_____
_____

Year _____

_____
_____
_____
_____

Year _____

_____
_____
_____
_____

Year _____

_____
_____
_____
_____

Year _____

_____
_____
_____
_____

February 24

Who is the last person to tell
you they loved you?

Year _____

_____
_____
_____
_____

Year _____

_____
_____
_____
_____

Year _____

_____
_____
_____
_____

Year _____

_____
_____
_____
_____

Year _____

_____
_____
_____
_____

February 25

If you could do today over, would
you change anything?

Year _____

_____
_____
_____
_____

Year _____

_____
_____
_____
_____

Year _____

_____
_____
_____
_____

Year _____

_____
_____
_____
_____

Year _____

_____
_____
_____
_____

February 26

What book are you reading right now?

Year _____

_____
_____
_____
_____

Year _____

_____
_____
_____
_____

Year _____

_____
_____
_____
_____

Year _____

_____
_____
_____
_____

Year _____

_____
_____
_____
_____

February 27

What stresses you?

Year _____

_____
_____
_____
_____

Year _____

_____
_____
_____
_____

Year _____

_____
_____
_____
_____

Year _____

_____
_____
_____
_____

Year _____

_____
_____
_____
_____

February 28

Did you learn any valuable
lessons today?

Year _____

_____
_____
_____
_____

Year _____

_____
_____
_____
_____

Year _____

_____
_____
_____
_____

Year _____

_____
_____
_____
_____

Year _____

_____
_____
_____
_____

February 29

What did you do to take
advantage of this extra day this year?

Year _____

_____
_____
_____
_____

Year _____

_____
_____
_____
_____

Year _____

_____
_____
_____
_____

Year _____

_____
_____
_____
_____

Year _____

_____
_____
_____
_____

March 1

Are you seeking security or adventure?

Year _____

_____
_____
_____
_____

Year _____

_____
_____
_____
_____

Year _____

_____
_____
_____
_____

Year _____

_____
_____
_____
_____

Year _____

_____
_____
_____
_____

March 2

—◦•◦—

Where do you want to travel next?

Year _____

_____
_____
_____
_____

Year _____

_____
_____
_____
_____

Year _____

_____
_____
_____
_____

Year _____

_____
_____
_____
_____

Year _____

_____
_____
_____
_____

_____ ❂ _____

March 3

What is the best place you have visited?

Year _____

_____
_____
_____
_____

Year _____

_____
_____
_____
_____

Year _____

_____
_____
_____
_____

Year _____

_____
_____
_____
_____

Year _____

_____
_____
_____
_____

March 4

What is the best experience you have ever done?

Year _____

_____
_____
_____
_____

Year _____

_____
_____
_____
_____

Year _____

_____
_____
_____
_____

Year _____

_____
_____
_____
_____

Year _____

_____
_____
_____
_____

March 5

What did you buy for yourself lately?

Year _____

_____
_____
_____
_____

Year _____

_____
_____
_____
_____

Year _____

_____
_____
_____
_____

Year _____

_____
_____
_____
_____

Year _____

_____
_____
_____
_____

March 6

What makes you feel safe?

Year _____

_____
_____
_____
_____

Year _____

_____
_____
_____
_____

Year _____

_____
_____
_____
_____

Year _____

_____
_____
_____
_____

Year _____

_____
_____
_____
_____

March 7

Where would you like to be at this time next year?

Year _____

_____
_____
_____
_____

Year _____

_____
_____
_____
_____

Year _____

_____
_____
_____
_____

Year _____

_____
_____
_____
_____

Year _____

_____
_____
_____
_____

March 8

What are your current short-term goals?

Year _____

_____
_____
_____
_____

Year _____

_____
_____
_____
_____

Year _____

_____
_____
_____
_____

Year _____

_____
_____
_____
_____

Year _____

_____
_____
_____
_____

March 9

What scares you the most?

Year _____

_____
_____
_____
_____

Year _____

_____
_____
_____
_____

Year _____

_____
_____
_____
_____

Year _____

_____
_____
_____
_____

Year _____

_____
_____
_____
_____

March 10

What is a risk you are too afraid to take? Why?

Year _____

_____
_____
_____
_____

Year _____

_____
_____
_____
_____

Year _____

_____
_____
_____
_____

Year _____

_____
_____
_____
_____

Year _____

_____
_____
_____
_____

March 11

What do you need more of in your life?

Year _____

_____
_____
_____
_____

Year _____

_____
_____
_____
_____

Year _____

_____
_____
_____
_____

Year _____

_____
_____
_____
_____

Year _____

_____
_____
_____

March 12

How did you change over the
last year?

Year _____

_____
_____
_____
_____

Year _____

_____
_____
_____
_____

Year _____

_____
_____
_____
_____

Year _____

_____
_____
_____
_____

Year _____

_____
_____
_____

March 13

Do you currently hold any grudges?

Year _____

_____
_____
_____
_____

Year _____

_____
_____
_____
_____

Year _____

_____
_____
_____
_____

Year _____

_____
_____
_____
_____

Year _____

_____
_____
_____
_____

March 14

Have you done anything you're proud of today?

Year _____

_____
_____
_____
_____

Year _____

_____
_____
_____
_____

Year _____

_____
_____
_____
_____

Year _____

_____
_____
_____
_____

Year _____

_____
_____
_____
_____

March 15

What are you really good at?

Year _____

_____
_____
_____
_____

Year _____

_____
_____
_____
_____

Year _____

_____
_____
_____
_____

Year _____

_____
_____
_____
_____

Year _____

_____
_____
_____
_____

March 16

What would you like to get better at?

Year _____

_____
_____
_____
_____

Year _____

_____
_____
_____
_____

Year _____

_____
_____
_____
_____

Year _____

_____
_____
_____
_____

Year _____

_____
_____
_____
_____

March 17

If you could have anything you wanted
right now, what would you ask for?

Year _____

_____
_____
_____
_____

Year _____

_____
_____
_____
_____

Year _____

_____
_____
_____
_____

Year _____

_____
_____
_____
_____

Year _____

_____
_____
_____
_____

March 18

---•◦•◦•---

If money was no object, what non-profit would you start?

Year _____

_____
_____
_____
_____

Year _____

_____
_____
_____
_____

Year _____

_____
_____
_____
_____

Year _____

_____
_____
_____
_____

Year _____

_____
_____
_____
_____

_____ ❧ _____

March 19

What can you do today to live a
better life tomorrow?

Year _____

_____
_____
_____
_____

Year _____

_____
_____
_____
_____

Year _____

_____
_____
_____
_____

Year _____

_____
_____
_____
_____

Year _____

_____
_____
_____
_____

March 20

—•◆•—

How has your day been?

Year _____

_____
_____
_____
_____

Year _____

_____
_____
_____
_____

Year _____

_____
_____
_____
_____

Year _____

_____
_____
_____
_____

Year _____

_____
_____
_____
_____

——— ❧ ———

March 21

What is your word for the year
and why?

Year _____
_____
_____
_____
_____

Year _____
_____
_____
_____
_____

Year _____
_____
_____
_____
_____

Year _____
_____
_____
_____
_____

Year _____
_____
_____
_____
_____

March 22

What new experience would you like to make?

Year _____

_____
_____
_____
_____

Year _____

_____
_____
_____
_____

Year _____

_____
_____
_____
_____

Year _____

_____
_____
_____
_____

Year _____

_____
_____
_____
_____

March 23

If you had to give a TED talk tomorrow,
what would it be about?

Year _____

_____
_____
_____
_____

Year _____

_____
_____
_____
_____

Year _____

_____
_____
_____
_____

Year _____

_____
_____
_____
_____

Year _____

_____
_____
_____

March 24

What is the best compliment you have ever received?

Year _____

_____
_____
_____
_____

Year _____

_____
_____
_____
_____

Year _____

_____
_____
_____
_____

Year _____

_____
_____
_____
_____

Year _____

_____
_____
_____
_____

March 25

What is one thing your life has in excess?

Year _____

_____
_____
_____
_____

Year _____

_____
_____
_____
_____

Year _____

_____
_____
_____
_____

Year _____

_____
_____
_____
_____

Year _____

_____
_____
_____
_____

March 26

What is something you should get rid off?

Year _____

_____
_____
_____
_____

Year _____

_____
_____
_____
_____

Year _____

_____
_____
_____
_____

Year _____

_____
_____
_____
_____

Year _____

_____
_____
_____
_____

March 27

How did you start your day, today?

Year _____

_____
_____
_____
_____

Year _____

_____
_____
_____
_____

Year _____

_____
_____
_____
_____

Year _____

_____
_____
_____
_____

Year _____

_____
_____
_____
_____

March 28

Do you collect anything?

Year _____

_____
_____
_____
_____

Year _____

_____
_____
_____
_____

Year _____

_____
_____
_____
_____

Year _____

_____
_____
_____
_____

Year _____

_____
_____
_____
_____

March 29

What are five things that make you smile?

Year _____

_____
_____
_____
_____

Year _____

_____
_____
_____
_____

Year _____

_____
_____
_____
_____

Year _____

_____
_____
_____
_____

Year _____

_____
_____
_____

March 30

What do you do to destress?

Year _____

_____
_____
_____
_____

Year _____

_____
_____
_____
_____

Year _____

_____
_____
_____
_____

Year _____

_____
_____
_____
_____

Year _____

_____
_____
_____
_____

March 31

Are you an early bird or night owl?

Year _____

_____
_____
_____
_____

Year _____

_____
_____
_____
_____

Year _____

_____
_____
_____
_____

Year _____

_____
_____
_____
_____

Year _____

_____
_____
_____
_____

April 1

Do you remember your last dream?

Year _____

_____
_____
_____
_____

Year _____

_____
_____
_____
_____

Year _____

_____
_____
_____
_____

Year _____

_____
_____
_____
_____

Year _____

_____
_____
_____
_____

April 2

What is your greatest strength?

Year _____
_____
_____
_____
_____

Year _____
_____
_____
_____
_____

Year _____
_____
_____
_____
_____

Year _____
_____
_____
_____
_____

Year _____
_____
_____
_____

April 3

———•◦•———

What is your greatest weakness?

Year _____

_____
_____
_____
_____

Year _____

_____
_____
_____
_____

Year _____

_____
_____
_____
_____

Year _____

_____
_____
_____
_____

Year _____

_____
_____
_____
_____

———❦———

April 4

How do you recharge?

Year _____

_____
_____
_____
_____

Year _____

_____
_____
_____
_____

Year _____

_____
_____
_____
_____

Year _____

_____
_____
_____
_____

Year _____

_____
_____
_____
_____

April 5

What song defines the past month?

Year _____

_____
_____
_____
_____

Year _____

_____
_____
_____
_____

Year _____

_____
_____
_____
_____

Year _____

_____
_____
_____
_____

Year _____

_____
_____
_____
_____

April 6

How do you measure your success?

Year _____

_____
_____
_____
_____

Year _____

_____
_____
_____
_____

Year _____

_____
_____
_____
_____

Year _____

_____
_____
_____
_____

Year _____

_____
_____
_____
_____

April 7

What do you like to do on rainy days?

Year _____

_____
_____
_____
_____

Year _____

_____
_____
_____
_____

Year _____

_____
_____
_____
_____

Year _____

_____
_____
_____
_____

Year _____

_____
_____
_____
_____

April 8

How easy/hard is it to
forgive yourself?

Year _____

_____
_____
_____
_____

Year _____

_____
_____
_____
_____

Year _____

_____
_____
_____
_____

Year _____

_____
_____
_____
_____

Year _____

_____
_____
_____
_____

April 9

What does "home" mean to you?

Year _____

_____
_____
_____
_____

Year _____

_____
_____
_____
_____

Year _____

_____
_____
_____
_____

Year _____

_____
_____
_____
_____

Year _____

_____
_____
_____
_____

April 10

An important decision you made recently?

Year _____

_____
_____
_____
_____

Year _____

_____
_____
_____
_____

Year _____

_____
_____
_____
_____

Year _____

_____
_____
_____
_____

Year _____

_____
_____
_____
_____

April 11

One thing you'd like to improve in yourself?

Year _____

_____
_____
_____
_____

Year _____

_____
_____
_____
_____

Year _____

_____
_____
_____
_____

Year _____

_____
_____
_____
_____

Year _____

_____
_____
_____
_____

April 12

What is your biggest dream?

Year _____

_____
_____
_____
_____

Year _____

_____
_____
_____
_____

Year _____

_____
_____
_____
_____

Year _____

_____
_____
_____
_____

Year _____

_____
_____
_____
_____

April 13

How is the weather today?

Year _____

_____
_____
_____
_____

Year _____

_____
_____
_____
_____

Year _____

_____
_____
_____
_____

Year _____

_____
_____
_____
_____

Year _____

_____
_____
_____

April 14

What's your goal for next week?

Year _____

_____
_____
_____
_____

Year _____

_____
_____
_____
_____

Year _____

_____
_____
_____
_____

Year _____

_____
_____
_____
_____

Year _____

_____
_____
_____
_____

April 15

What did you do today that
brought you closer to your dream?

Year _____

_____
_____
_____
_____

Year _____

_____
_____
_____
_____

Year _____

_____
_____
_____
_____

Year _____

_____
_____
_____
_____

Year _____

_____
_____
_____
_____

April 16

One behavior you need to let go?

Year _____

_____
_____
_____
_____

Year _____

_____
_____
_____
_____

Year _____

_____
_____
_____
_____

Year _____

_____
_____
_____
_____

Year _____

_____
_____
_____
_____

April 17

Who is someone that inspires you and why?

Year _____

_____
_____
_____
_____

Year _____

_____
_____
_____
_____

Year _____

_____
_____
_____
_____

Year _____

_____
_____
_____
_____

Year _____

_____
_____
_____
_____

April 18

What song is in your mind?

Year _____

_____
_____
_____
_____

Year _____

_____
_____
_____
_____

Year _____

_____
_____
_____
_____

Year _____

_____
_____
_____
_____

Year _____

_____
_____
_____
_____

April 19

What book are you reading right now?

Year _____

_____
_____
_____
_____

Year _____

_____
_____
_____
_____

Year _____

_____
_____
_____
_____

Year _____

_____
_____
_____
_____

Year _____

_____
_____
_____
_____

April 20

What was your latest success?

Year _____

_____
_____
_____
_____

Year _____

_____
_____
_____
_____

Year _____

_____
_____
_____
_____

Year _____

_____
_____
_____
_____

Year _____

_____
_____
_____
_____

April 21

What are some of the biggest
rewards of your day to day life?

Year _____

_____
_____
_____
_____

Year _____

_____
_____
_____
_____

Year _____

_____
_____
_____
_____

Year _____

_____
_____
_____
_____

Year _____

_____
_____
_____
_____

April 22

What's on your mind right now?

Year _____

_____
_____
_____
_____

Year _____

_____
_____
_____
_____

Year _____

_____
_____
_____
_____

Year _____

_____
_____
_____
_____

Year _____

_____
_____
_____
_____

April 23

What would you like to eat today?

Year _____

_____
_____
_____
_____

Year _____

_____
_____
_____
_____

Year _____

_____
_____
_____
_____

Year _____

_____
_____
_____
_____

Year _____

_____
_____
_____
_____

April 24

Where do you want to be in 5 years?

Year _____

_____
_____
_____
_____

Year _____

_____
_____
_____
_____

Year _____

_____
_____
_____
_____

Year _____

_____
_____
_____
_____

Year _____

_____
_____
_____
_____

April 25

How does your schedule look like today?

Year _____

_____
_____
_____
_____

Year _____

_____
_____
_____
_____

Year _____

_____
_____
_____
_____

Year _____

_____
_____
_____
_____

Year _____

_____
_____
_____
_____

April 26

Most expensive possession you own?

Year _____

_____
_____
_____
_____

Year _____

_____
_____
_____
_____

Year _____

_____
_____
_____
_____

Year _____

_____
_____
_____
_____

Year _____

_____
_____
_____
_____

April 27

I really wish...

Year _____

_____
_____
_____
_____

Year _____

_____
_____
_____
_____

Year _____

_____
_____
_____
_____

Year _____

_____
_____
_____
_____

Year _____

_____
_____
_____
_____

April 28

When was the last time you visualized
yourself achieving your dreams?

Year _____

_____
_____
_____
_____

Year _____

_____
_____
_____
_____

Year _____

_____
_____
_____
_____

Year _____

_____
_____
_____
_____

Year _____

_____
_____
_____
_____

April 29

How would you describe your ability
to manage stress?

Year _____

_____
_____
_____
_____

Year _____

_____
_____
_____
_____

Year _____

_____
_____
_____
_____

Year _____

_____
_____
_____
_____

Year _____

_____
_____
_____
_____

April 30

What word do you say the most?

Year _____

_____
_____
_____
_____

Year _____

_____
_____
_____
_____

Year _____

_____
_____
_____
_____

Year _____

_____
_____
_____
_____

Year _____

_____
_____
_____
_____

May 1

What's more important to you:
personal life or professional career?

Year _____

_____
_____
_____
_____

Year _____

_____
_____
_____
_____

Year _____

_____
_____
_____
_____

Year _____

_____
_____
_____
_____

Year _____

_____
_____
_____
_____

May 2

How important is physical
activity in your life?

Year _____

_____
_____
_____
_____

Year _____

_____
_____
_____
_____

Year _____

_____
_____
_____
_____

Year _____

_____
_____
_____
_____

Year _____

_____
_____
_____
_____

May 3

Are you afraid of leaving your comfort zone?

Year _____

_____
_____
_____
_____

Year _____

_____
_____
_____
_____

Year _____

_____
_____
_____
_____

Year _____

_____
_____
_____
_____

Year _____

_____
_____
_____
_____

May 4

What challenges have you overcome
recently and how did you do it?

Year _____

_____
_____
_____
_____

Year _____

_____
_____
_____
_____

Year _____

_____
_____
_____
_____

Year _____

_____
_____
_____
_____

Year _____

_____
_____
_____
_____

May 5

When do you feel lonely?

Year _____

_____
_____
_____
_____

Year _____

_____
_____
_____
_____

Year _____

_____
_____
_____
_____

Year _____

_____
_____
_____
_____

Year _____

_____
_____
_____
_____

May 6

Read a book or watch a movie?

Year _____

_____
_____
_____
_____

Year _____

_____
_____
_____
_____

Year _____

_____
_____
_____
_____

Year _____

_____
_____
_____
_____

Year _____

_____
_____
_____
_____

May 7

Do you find it easy to stand up for yourself?

Year _____

_____
_____
_____
_____

Year _____

_____
_____
_____
_____

Year _____

_____
_____
_____
_____

Year _____

_____
_____
_____
_____

Year _____

_____
_____
_____
_____

May 8

Who's the most important person in
your life right now?

Year _____

_____
_____
_____
_____

Year _____

_____
_____
_____
_____

Year _____

_____
_____
_____
_____

Year _____

_____
_____
_____
_____

Year _____

_____
_____
_____
_____

May 9

Do you find it important to
keep up with technology?

Year _____

_____
_____
_____
_____

Year _____

_____
_____
_____
_____

Year _____

_____
_____
_____
_____

Year _____

_____
_____
_____
_____

Year _____

_____
_____
_____
_____

May 10

Your favorite small pleasure?

Year _____

_____
_____
_____
_____

Year _____

_____
_____
_____
_____

Year _____

_____
_____
_____
_____

Year _____

_____
_____
_____
_____

Year _____

_____
_____
_____
_____

May 11

How much time do you spend daily watching TV?

Year _____

_____
_____
_____
_____

Year _____

_____
_____
_____
_____

Year _____

_____
_____
_____
_____

Year _____

_____
_____
_____
_____

Year _____

_____
_____
_____
_____

May 12

Name one of your skills you'd like
to teach others.

Year _____

_____
_____
_____
_____

Year _____

_____
_____
_____
_____

Year _____

_____
_____
_____
_____

Year _____

_____
_____
_____
_____

Year _____

_____
_____
_____
_____

May 13

How do you feel when you can't tick
off everything on your to-do list?

Year _____

_____
_____
_____
_____

Year _____

_____
_____
_____
_____

Year _____

_____
_____
_____
_____

Year _____

_____
_____
_____
_____

Year _____

_____
_____
_____
_____

May 14

One piece of advice to your younger self.

Year _____

_____
_____
_____
_____

Year _____

_____
_____
_____
_____

Year _____

_____
_____
_____
_____

Year _____

_____
_____
_____
_____

Year _____

_____
_____
_____
_____

May 15

Next year today i will be/have....

Year _____

_____
_____
_____
_____

Year _____

_____
_____
_____
_____

Year _____

_____
_____
_____
_____

Year _____

_____
_____
_____
_____

Year _____

_____
_____
_____
_____

May 16

Favorite part of your body and why.

Year _____

_____
_____
_____
_____

Year _____

_____
_____
_____
_____

Year _____

_____
_____
_____
_____

Year _____

_____
_____
_____
_____

Year _____

_____
_____
_____

May 17

Something you're thankful for.

Year _____

_____
_____
_____
_____

Year _____

_____
_____
_____
_____

Year _____

_____
_____
_____
_____

Year _____

_____
_____
_____
_____

Year _____

_____
_____
_____
_____

May 18

What color relates to the way you feel right now?

Year _____

_____
_____
_____
_____

Year _____

_____
_____
_____
_____

Year _____

_____
_____
_____
_____

Year _____

_____
_____
_____
_____

Year _____

_____
_____
_____
_____

May 19

What's your most incredible and scary dream?

Year _____

_____
_____
_____
_____

Year _____

_____
_____
_____
_____

Year _____

_____
_____
_____
_____

Year _____

_____
_____
_____
_____

Year _____

_____
_____
_____
_____

May 20

An accomplishment that makes you proud of yourself.

Year _____

_____
_____
_____
_____

Year _____

_____
_____
_____
_____

Year _____

_____
_____
_____
_____

Year _____

_____
_____
_____
_____

Year _____

_____
_____
_____
_____

May 21

How would you describe your alarm clock?

Year _____

_____
_____
_____
_____

Year _____

_____
_____
_____
_____

Year _____

_____
_____
_____
_____

Year _____

_____
_____
_____
_____

Year _____

_____
_____
_____
_____

May 22

How do you plan to achieve your main Goal?

Year _____

_____
_____
_____
_____

Year _____

_____
_____
_____
_____

Year _____

_____
_____
_____
_____

Year _____

_____
_____
_____
_____

Year _____

_____
_____
_____
_____

May 23

Who are the 5 people you spend most of your time with?

Year _____

_____
_____
_____
_____

Year _____

_____
_____
_____
_____

Year _____

_____
_____
_____
_____

Year _____

_____
_____
_____
_____

Year _____

_____
_____
_____
_____

May 24

Who do you look up to?

Year _____

_____
_____
_____
_____

Year _____

_____
_____
_____
_____

Year _____

_____
_____
_____
_____

Year _____

_____
_____
_____
_____

Year _____

_____
_____
_____
_____

May 25

Are you easily influenced by other people?

Year _____

_____
_____
_____
_____

Year _____

_____
_____
_____
_____

Year _____

_____
_____
_____
_____

Year _____

_____
_____
_____
_____

Year _____

_____
_____
_____
_____

May 26

What are your 5 core values?

Year _____
_____
_____
_____
_____

Year _____
_____
_____
_____
_____

Year _____
_____
_____
_____
_____

Year _____
_____
_____
_____
_____

Year _____
_____
_____
_____
_____

May 27

What drains
the most energy from you?

Year _____

_____
_____
_____
_____

Year _____

_____
_____
_____
_____

Year _____

_____
_____
_____
_____

Year _____

_____
_____
_____
_____

Year _____

_____
_____
_____

May 28

Do you get your energy from being around
other people or spending time alone?

Year _____

_____
_____
_____
_____

Year _____

_____
_____
_____
_____

Year _____

_____
_____
_____
_____

Year _____

_____
_____
_____
_____

Year _____

_____
_____
_____
_____

May 29

How often do you have "me time"?

Year _____

_____
_____
_____
_____

Year _____

_____
_____
_____
_____

Year _____

_____
_____
_____
_____

Year _____

_____
_____
_____
_____

Year _____

_____
_____
_____
_____

May 30

What are you good at?

Year _____

_____
_____
_____
_____

Year _____

_____
_____
_____
_____

Year _____

_____
_____
_____
_____

Year _____

_____
_____
_____
_____

Year _____

_____
_____
_____
_____

May 31

What have you given up on?

Year _____

_____
_____
_____
_____

Year _____

_____
_____
_____
_____

Year _____

_____
_____
_____
_____

Year _____

_____
_____
_____
_____

Year _____

_____
_____
_____
_____

June 1

What do you
take for granted in your life?

Year _____

_____
_____
_____
_____

Year _____

_____
_____
_____
_____

Year _____

_____
_____
_____
_____

Year _____

_____
_____
_____
_____

Year _____

_____
_____
_____
_____

June 2

Why are you passionate about what you do?

Year _____

_____
_____
_____
_____

Year _____

_____
_____
_____
_____

Year _____

_____
_____
_____
_____

Year _____

_____
_____
_____
_____

Year _____

_____
_____
_____
_____

June 3

Is there something, that keeps you up worrying?

Year _____

_____
_____
_____
_____

Year _____

_____
_____
_____
_____

Year _____

_____
_____
_____
_____

Year _____

_____
_____
_____
_____

Year _____

_____
_____
_____
_____

June 4

Do you wake up excited to start the day?

Year _____

_____
_____
_____
_____

Year _____

_____
_____
_____
_____

Year _____

_____
_____
_____
_____

Year _____

_____
_____
_____
_____

Year _____

_____
_____
_____
_____

June 5

How did you picture yourself at your actual age, when you were a child?

Year _____

_____
_____
_____
_____

Year _____

_____
_____
_____
_____

Year _____

_____
_____
_____
_____

Year _____

_____
_____
_____
_____

Year _____

_____
_____
_____
_____

June 6

Do you live in the past, present, or future?

Year _____

_____
_____
_____
_____

Year _____

_____
_____
_____
_____

Year _____

_____
_____
_____
_____

Year _____

_____
_____
_____
_____

Year _____

_____
_____
_____

June 7

Do you need to let go of something?

Year _____

_____
_____
_____
_____

Year _____

_____
_____
_____
_____

Year _____

_____
_____
_____
_____

Year _____

_____
_____
_____
_____

Year _____

_____
_____
_____
_____

June 8

What is your
favorite topic to talk about?

Year _____

_____
_____
_____
_____

Year _____

_____
_____
_____
_____

Year _____

_____
_____
_____
_____

Year _____

_____
_____
_____
_____

Year _____

_____
_____
_____
_____

June 9

If you could go anywhere in the world
right now, where would you go?

Year _____

_____
_____
_____
_____

Year _____

_____
_____
_____
_____

Year _____

_____
_____
_____
_____

Year _____

_____
_____
_____
_____

Year _____

_____
_____
_____
_____

June 10

Are you happy with your life?

Year _____

_____
_____
_____
_____

Year _____

_____
_____
_____
_____

Year _____

_____
_____
_____
_____

Year _____

_____
_____
_____
_____

Year _____

_____
_____
_____
_____

June 11

Which phase do you think was the best phase of your life?

Year _____

_____
_____
_____
_____

Year _____

_____
_____
_____
_____

Year _____

_____
_____
_____
_____

Year _____

_____
_____
_____
_____

Year _____

_____
_____
_____
_____

June 12

What do you think was the worst phase of your life?

Year _____

_____
_____
_____
_____

Year _____

_____
_____
_____
_____

Year _____

_____
_____
_____
_____

Year _____

_____
_____
_____
_____

Year _____

_____
_____
_____
_____

June 13

Have you ever lost someone who
was very close to you?

Year _____

_____
_____
_____
_____

Year _____

_____
_____
_____
_____

Year _____

_____
_____
_____
_____

Year _____

_____
_____
_____
_____

Year _____

_____
_____
_____
_____

June 14

What would you say to that person if you could see her/him now?

Year _____

_____
_____
_____
_____

Year _____

_____
_____
_____
_____

Year _____

_____
_____
_____
_____

Year _____

_____
_____
_____
_____

Year _____

_____
_____
_____
_____

June 15

What is that one thing that people don't know about you?

Year _____

_____
_____
_____
_____

Year _____

_____
_____
_____
_____

Year _____

_____
_____
_____
_____

Year _____

_____
_____
_____
_____

Year _____

_____
_____
_____
_____

June 16

Why don't they know it?

Year _____

_____
_____
_____
_____

Year _____

_____
_____
_____
_____

Year _____

_____
_____
_____
_____

Year _____

_____
_____
_____
_____

Year _____

_____
_____
_____
_____

June 17

Which things do you want to check off
of your bucket list this year?

Year _____

_____
_____
_____
_____

Year _____

_____
_____
_____
_____

Year _____

_____
_____
_____
_____

Year _____

_____
_____
_____
_____

Year _____

_____
_____
_____
_____

June 18

When have you experienced the
most intense adrenaline rush?

Year _____

_____
_____
_____
_____

Year _____

_____
_____
_____
_____

Year _____

_____
_____
_____
_____

Year _____

_____
_____
_____
_____

Year _____

_____
_____
_____
_____

June 19

What is the craziest thing you have done in your life, and if you get a chance, would you do it again?

Year _____

_____
_____
_____
_____

Year _____

_____
_____
_____
_____

Year _____

_____
_____
_____
_____

Year _____

_____
_____
_____
_____

Year _____

_____
_____
_____
_____

June 20

What do you think about the most
when you are alone?

Year _____

_____
_____
_____
_____

Year _____

_____
_____
_____
_____

Year _____

_____
_____
_____
_____

Year _____

_____
_____
_____
_____

Year _____

_____
_____
_____
_____

June 21

Which book had the biggest impact
on your life? Why?

Year _____

_____
_____
_____
_____

Year _____

_____
_____
_____
_____

Year _____

_____
_____
_____
_____

Year _____

_____
_____
_____
_____

Year _____

_____
_____
_____

June 22

Which movie had the biggest impact
on your life? Why?

Year _____

_____
_____
_____
_____

Year _____

_____
_____
_____
_____

Year _____

_____
_____
_____
_____

Year _____

_____
_____
_____
_____

Year _____

_____
_____
_____
_____

June 23

What is the biggest lie you have ever told?

Year _____

_____
_____
_____
_____

Year _____

_____
_____
_____
_____

Year _____

_____
_____
_____
_____

Year _____

_____
_____
_____
_____

Year _____

_____
_____
_____
_____

June 24

Who do you envy the most?

Year _____

_____
_____
_____
_____

Year _____

_____
_____
_____
_____

Year _____

_____
_____
_____
_____

Year _____

_____
_____
_____
_____

Year _____

_____
_____
_____
_____

June 25

If you were an animal, which animal would you be?

Year _____

_____
_____
_____
_____

Year _____

_____
_____
_____
_____

Year _____

_____
_____
_____
_____

Year _____

_____
_____
_____
_____

Year _____

_____
_____
_____
_____

June 26

What age do you feel?

Year _____

_____
_____
_____
_____

Year _____

_____
_____
_____
_____

Year _____

_____
_____
_____
_____

Year _____

_____
_____
_____
_____

Year _____

_____
_____
_____
_____

June 27

What change do you want to make?

Year _____

_____
_____
_____
_____

Year _____

_____
_____
_____
_____

Year _____

_____
_____
_____
_____

Year _____

_____
_____
_____
_____

Year _____

_____
_____
_____

June 28

What famous person would you like to meet? Why?

Year _____

_____
_____
_____
_____

Year _____

_____
_____
_____
_____

Year _____

_____
_____
_____
_____

Year _____

_____
_____
_____
_____

Year _____

_____
_____
_____
_____

June 29

Who was especially kind to you today?

Year _____

_____
_____
_____
_____

Year _____

_____
_____
_____
_____

Year _____

_____
_____
_____
_____

Year _____

_____
_____
_____
_____

Year _____

_____
_____
_____
_____

June 30

When was the last time you said your
parents you love them?

Year _____

_____
_____
_____
_____

Year _____

_____
_____
_____
_____

Year _____

_____
_____
_____
_____

Year _____

_____
_____
_____
_____

Year _____

_____
_____
_____
_____

July 1

What lie have you told recently?

Year _____
_____
_____
_____
_____

Year _____
_____
_____
_____
_____

Year _____
_____
_____
_____
_____

Year _____
_____
_____
_____
_____

Year _____
_____
_____
_____
_____

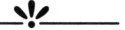

July 2

What are you beginning to doubt?

Year _____

_____
_____
_____
_____

Year _____

_____
_____
_____
_____

Year _____

_____
_____
_____
_____

Year _____

_____
_____
_____
_____

Year _____

_____
_____
_____
_____

July 3

How hard did you work today?

Year _____

_____
_____
_____
_____
_____

Year _____

_____
_____
_____
_____
_____

Year _____

_____
_____
_____
_____
_____

Year _____

_____
_____
_____
_____
_____

Year _____

_____
_____
_____
_____
_____

July 4

What job would you like to trade your job
for this week?

Year _____

_____
_____
_____
_____

Year _____

_____
_____
_____
_____

Year _____

_____
_____
_____
_____

Year _____

_____
_____
_____
_____

Year _____

_____
_____
_____
_____

July 5

If your house was on fire, which object would you try to save?

Year _____

_____
_____
_____
_____

Year _____

_____
_____
_____
_____

Year _____

_____
_____
_____
_____

Year _____

_____
_____
_____
_____

Year _____

_____
_____
_____
_____

July 6

If you could only take 3 things on a desert island, what would they be?

Year _____

_____
_____
_____
_____

Year _____

_____
_____
_____
_____

Year _____

_____
_____
_____
_____

Year _____

_____
_____
_____
_____

Year _____

_____
_____
_____
_____

July 7

Who are the people in your life that really understand you?

Year _____

_____
_____
_____
_____

Year _____

_____
_____
_____
_____

Year _____

_____
_____
_____
_____

Year _____

_____
_____
_____
_____

Year _____

_____
_____
_____
_____

July 8

How many real friends do you have?

Year _____

_____
_____
_____
_____

Year _____

_____
_____
_____
_____

Year _____

_____
_____
_____
_____

Year _____

_____
_____
_____
_____

Year _____

_____
_____
_____
_____

July 9

What could you never give up?

Year _____

_____
_____
_____
_____

Year _____

_____
_____
_____
_____

Year _____

_____
_____
_____
_____

Year _____

_____
_____
_____
_____

Year _____

_____
_____
_____
_____

July 10

What is one mistake you don't regret making?

Year _____

_____
_____
_____
_____

Year _____

_____
_____
_____
_____

Year _____

_____
_____
_____
_____

Year _____

_____
_____
_____
_____

Year _____

_____
_____
_____
_____

July 11

Which instrument would you like to learn how to play?

Year _____

_____
_____
_____
_____

Year _____

_____
_____
_____
_____

Year _____

_____
_____
_____
_____

Year _____

_____
_____
_____
_____

Year _____

_____
_____
_____
_____

July 12

What is the best part of your day?

Year _____

_____
_____
_____
_____

Year _____

_____
_____
_____
_____

Year _____

_____
_____
_____
_____

Year _____

_____
_____
_____
_____

Year _____

_____
_____
_____
_____

July 13

What relationship in your life you wish you could improve?

Year _____

_____
_____
_____
_____

Year _____

_____
_____
_____
_____

Year _____

_____
_____
_____
_____

Year _____

_____
_____
_____
_____

Year _____

_____
_____
_____
_____

July 14

If you could rename yourself, which name would you choose?

Year _____

_____
_____
_____
_____

Year _____

_____
_____
_____
_____

Year _____

_____
_____
_____
_____

Year _____

_____
_____
_____
_____

Year _____

_____
_____
_____
_____

July 15

If you could live during any time
period, which one would you choose?

Year _____

_____
_____
_____
_____

Year _____

_____
_____
_____
_____

Year _____

_____
_____
_____
_____

Year _____

_____
_____
_____
_____

Year _____

_____
_____
_____

July 16

What food are you craving right now?

Year _____

_____
_____
_____
_____

Year _____

_____
_____
_____
_____

Year _____

_____
_____
_____
_____

Year _____

_____
_____
_____
_____

Year _____

_____
_____
_____
_____

July 17

If you won a million dollar, what would you buy first?

Year _____

_____
_____
_____
_____

Year _____

_____
_____
_____
_____

Year _____

_____
_____
_____
_____

Year _____

_____
_____
_____
_____

Year _____

_____
_____
_____
_____

July 18

What are you shy about?

Year _____

_____
_____
_____
_____

Year _____

_____
_____
_____
_____

Year _____

_____
_____
_____
_____

Year _____

_____
_____
_____
_____

Year _____

_____
_____
_____
_____

July 19

When was the last time you were really angry?

Year _____

_____
_____
_____
_____

Year _____

_____
_____
_____
_____

Year _____

_____
_____
_____
_____

Year _____

_____
_____
_____
_____

Year _____

_____
_____
_____
_____

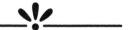

July 20

On what do you spend too much money?

Year _____

_____
_____
_____
_____

Year _____

_____
_____
_____
_____

Year _____

_____
_____
_____
_____

Year _____

_____
_____
_____
_____

Year _____

_____
_____
_____
_____

July 21

When was the last time you cried?

Year _____

_____
_____
_____
_____

Year _____

_____
_____
_____
_____

Year _____

_____
_____
_____
_____

Year _____

_____
_____
_____
_____

Year _____

_____
_____
_____
_____

July 22

What do you see outside of your window?

Year _____

_____
_____
_____
_____

Year _____

_____
_____
_____
_____

Year _____

_____
_____
_____
_____

Year _____

_____
_____
_____
_____

Year _____

_____
_____
_____
_____

July 23

How many new places have you
visited this year?

Year _____

_____
_____
_____
_____

Year _____

_____
_____
_____
_____

Year _____

_____
_____
_____
_____

Year _____

_____
_____
_____
_____

Year _____

_____
_____
_____
_____

July 24

What promise have you kept?

Year _____

_____
_____
_____
_____

Year _____

_____
_____
_____
_____

Year _____

_____
_____
_____
_____

Year _____

_____
_____
_____
_____

Year _____

_____
_____
_____
_____

July 25

What is the first thing you did this morning?

Year _____

_____
_____
_____
_____

Year _____

_____
_____
_____
_____

Year _____

_____
_____
_____
_____

Year _____

_____
_____
_____
_____

Year _____

_____
_____
_____
_____

July 26

How famous would you like to be?

Year _____

_____
_____
_____
_____

Year _____

_____
_____
_____
_____

Year _____

_____
_____
_____
_____

Year _____

_____
_____
_____
_____

Year _____

_____
_____
_____
_____

July 27

What is your favorite day of the week and why?

Year _____
_____
_____
_____
_____

Year _____
_____
_____
_____
_____

Year _____
_____
_____
_____
_____

Year _____
_____
_____
_____
_____

Year _____
_____
_____
_____
_____

July 28

What about your life is different than you expected to be?

Year _____

_____
_____
_____
_____

Year _____

_____
_____
_____
_____

Year _____

_____
_____
_____
_____

Year _____

_____
_____
_____
_____

Year _____

_____
_____
_____
_____

July 29

Who was the last person you talked to on the phone?

Year _____

_____
_____
_____
_____

Year _____

_____
_____
_____
_____

Year _____

_____
_____
_____
_____

Year _____

_____
_____
_____
_____

Year _____

_____
_____
_____
_____

July 30

Do you feel blessed or cursed?

Year _____

_____
_____
_____
_____

Year _____

_____
_____
_____
_____

Year _____

_____
_____
_____
_____

Year _____

_____
_____
_____
_____

Year _____

_____
_____
_____
_____

July 31

Who always has your support?

Year _____

_____
_____
_____
_____

Year _____

_____
_____
_____
_____

Year _____

_____
_____
_____
_____

Year _____

_____
_____
_____
_____

Year _____

_____
_____
_____
_____

August 1

Who always supports you?

Year _____

_____
_____
_____
_____

Year _____

_____
_____
_____
_____

Year _____

_____
_____
_____
_____

Year _____

_____
_____
_____
_____

Year _____

_____
_____
_____
_____

August 2

On which topic do you consider yourself an expert?

Year _____

_____
_____
_____
_____

Year _____

_____
_____
_____
_____

Year _____

_____
_____
_____
_____

Year _____

_____
_____
_____
_____

Year _____

_____
_____
_____
_____

August 3

What TV show always makes you laugh?

Year _____

_____
_____
_____
_____

Year _____

_____
_____
_____
_____

Year _____

_____
_____
_____
_____

Year _____

_____
_____
_____
_____

Year _____

_____
_____
_____
_____

August 4

What is your dream house?

Year _____
_____
_____
_____
_____

Year _____
_____
_____
_____
_____

Year _____
_____
_____
_____
_____

Year _____
_____
_____
_____
_____

Year _____
_____
_____
_____
_____

August 5

What hasn't changed about you over the years?

Year _____

_____
_____
_____
_____

Year _____

_____
_____
_____
_____

Year _____

_____
_____
_____
_____

Year _____

_____
_____
_____
_____

Year _____

_____
_____
_____
_____

August 6

What is on your bedside table right now?

Year _____

_____
_____
_____
_____

Year _____

_____
_____
_____
_____

Year _____

_____
_____
_____
_____

Year _____

_____
_____
_____
_____

Year _____

_____
_____
_____
_____

August 7

What makes you feel like a kid again?

Year _____

_____
_____
_____
_____

Year _____

_____
_____
_____
_____

Year _____

_____
_____
_____
_____

Year _____

_____
_____
_____
_____

Year _____

_____
_____
_____
_____

August 8

What are you looking forward to?

Year _____

_____
_____
_____
_____

Year _____

_____
_____
_____
_____

Year _____

_____
_____
_____
_____

Year _____

_____
_____
_____
_____

Year _____

_____
_____
_____

August 9

What do you love about your life?

Year _____

_____
_____
_____
_____

Year _____

_____
_____
_____
_____

Year _____

_____
_____
_____
_____

Year _____

_____
_____
_____
_____

Year _____

_____
_____
_____
_____

August 10

One thing you dislike.

Year _____

_____
_____
_____
_____

Year _____

_____
_____
_____
_____

Year _____

_____
_____
_____
_____

Year _____

_____
_____
_____
_____

Year _____

_____
_____
_____
_____

August 11

When are you the happiest version of you?

Year _____

_____
_____
_____

Year _____

_____
_____
_____
_____

Year _____

_____
_____
_____
_____

Year _____

_____
_____
_____
_____

Year _____

_____
_____
_____

August 12

How can you add to your happiness?

Year _____
_____
_____
_____
_____

Year _____
_____
_____
_____
_____

Year _____
_____
_____
_____
_____

Year _____
_____
_____
_____
_____

Year _____
_____
_____
_____
_____

August 13

What needs to happen today to make
your day perfect?

Year _____

_____
_____
_____
_____

Year _____

_____
_____
_____
_____

Year _____

_____
_____
_____
_____

Year _____

_____
_____
_____
_____

Year _____

_____
_____
_____
_____

August 14

What are you wearing right now?

Year _____

_____
_____
_____
_____

Year _____

_____
_____
_____
_____

Year _____

_____
_____
_____
_____

Year _____

_____
_____
_____
_____

Year _____

_____
_____
_____
_____

August 15

How do you feel
about last-minute changes?

Year _____

_____
_____
_____
_____

Year _____

_____
_____
_____
_____

Year _____

_____
_____
_____
_____

Year _____

_____
_____
_____
_____

Year _____

_____
_____
_____
_____

August 16

What is your favorite sport?

Year _____

_____
_____
_____
_____

Year _____

_____
_____
_____
_____

Year _____

_____
_____
_____
_____

Year _____

_____
_____
_____
_____

Year _____

_____
_____
_____
_____

August 17

How frequently do you exercise?

Year _____

_____
_____
_____
_____

Year _____

_____
_____
_____
_____

Year _____

_____
_____
_____
_____

Year _____

_____
_____
_____
_____

Year _____

_____
_____
_____
_____

August 18

How do you deal with peer pressure?

Year _____

_____
_____
_____
_____

Year _____

_____
_____
_____
_____

Year _____

_____
_____
_____
_____

Year _____

_____
_____
_____
_____

Year _____

_____
_____
_____
_____

August 19

What's your view on self-love?

Year _____

_____
_____
_____
_____

Year _____

_____
_____
_____
_____

Year _____

_____
_____
_____
_____

Year _____

_____
_____
_____
_____

Year _____

_____
_____
_____
_____

August 20

How hard is it for you to say "no"?

Year _____

_____
_____
_____
_____

Year _____

_____
_____
_____
_____

Year _____

_____
_____
_____
_____

Year _____

_____
_____
_____
_____

Year _____

_____
_____
_____
_____

August 21

What do you think about multitasking?

Year _____

_____

_____

_____

Year _____

_____

_____

_____

_____

Year _____

_____

_____

_____

_____

Year _____

_____

_____

_____

_____

Year _____

_____

_____

_____

_____

August 22

What motivates you?

Year _____

_____
_____
_____
_____

Year _____

_____
_____
_____
_____

Year _____

_____
_____
_____
_____

Year _____

_____
_____
_____
_____

Year _____

_____
_____
_____
_____

August 23

Your mindset today.

Year _____

_____
_____
_____
_____

Year _____

_____
_____
_____
_____

Year _____

_____
_____
_____
_____

Year _____

_____
_____
_____
_____

Year _____

_____
_____
_____
_____

August 24

What do you generally do before going to bed?

Year _____

_____
_____
_____
_____

Year _____

_____
_____
_____
_____

Year _____

_____
_____
_____
_____

Year _____

_____
_____
_____
_____

Year _____

_____
_____
_____
_____

August 25

What do you love about your job/career?

Year _____

_____
_____
_____
_____

Year _____

_____
_____
_____
_____

Year _____

_____
_____
_____
_____

Year _____

_____
_____
_____
_____

Year _____

_____
_____
_____
_____

August 26

One fun fact about yourself.

Year _____

_____
_____
_____
_____

Year _____

_____
_____
_____
_____

Year _____

_____
_____
_____
_____

Year _____

_____
_____
_____
_____

Year _____

_____
_____
_____
_____

August 27

An event you'll remember your entire life.

Year _____

_____
_____
_____
_____

Year _____

_____
_____
_____
_____

Year _____

_____
_____
_____
_____

Year _____

_____
_____
_____
_____

Year _____

_____
_____
_____
_____

August 28

Describe the lifestyle of your Dreams.

Year _____

_____
_____
_____
_____

Year _____

_____
_____
_____
_____

Year _____

_____
_____
_____
_____

Year _____

_____
_____
_____
_____

Year _____

_____
_____
_____
_____

August 29

Random act of kindness you practiced
today.

Year _____

_____
_____
_____
_____

Year _____

_____
_____
_____
_____

Year _____

_____
_____
_____
_____

Year _____

_____
_____
_____
_____

Year _____

_____
_____
_____
_____

August 30

Scariest thing you have ever done.

Year _____

_____
_____
_____
_____

Year _____

_____
_____
_____
_____

Year _____

_____
_____
_____
_____

Year _____

_____
_____
_____
_____

Year _____

_____
_____
_____
_____

August 31

Your favorite memory from your school years.

Year _____

_____
_____
_____
_____

Year _____

_____
_____
_____
_____

Year _____

_____
_____
_____
_____

Year _____

_____
_____
_____
_____

Year _____

_____
_____
_____
_____

September 1

If you were to write a
book, what would it be about?

Year _____

_____
_____
_____
_____

Year _____

_____
_____
_____
_____

Year _____

_____
_____
_____
_____

Year _____

_____
_____
_____
_____

Year _____

_____
_____
_____

September 2

How good are you in keeping secrets?

Year _____

_____
_____
_____

Year _____

_____
_____
_____
_____

Year _____

_____
_____
_____
_____

Year _____

_____
_____
_____
_____

Year _____

_____
_____
_____
_____

September 3

Are you keeping a big secret right now?

Year _____

_____
_____
_____
_____

Year _____

_____
_____
_____
_____

Year _____

_____
_____
_____
_____

Year _____

_____
_____
_____
_____

Year _____

_____
_____
_____
_____

September 4

What animal would you like to see in their natural habitat?

Year _____

_____
_____
_____
_____

Year _____

_____
_____
_____
_____

Year _____

_____
_____
_____
_____

Year _____

_____
_____
_____
_____

Year _____

_____
_____
_____
_____

September 5

How do you feel when you're asked to speak in public?

Year _____

_____
_____
_____
_____

Year _____

_____
_____
_____
_____

Year _____

_____
_____
_____
_____

Year _____

_____
_____
_____
_____

Year _____

_____
_____
_____
_____

September 6

Consumerism or minimalism?

Year _____

_____
_____
_____
_____
_____

Year _____

_____
_____
_____
_____
_____

Year _____

_____
_____
_____
_____
_____

Year _____

_____
_____
_____
_____
_____

Year _____

_____
_____
_____
_____
_____

September 7

For how long would you stay on a desert island?

Year _____

_____
_____
_____
_____

Year _____

_____
_____
_____
_____

Year _____

_____
_____
_____
_____

Year _____

_____
_____
_____
_____

Year _____

_____
_____
_____
_____

September 8

What's the most
interesting place you've ever been to?

Year _____

_____
_____
_____
_____

Year _____

_____
_____
_____
_____

Year _____

_____
_____
_____
_____

Year _____

_____
_____
_____
_____

Year _____

_____
_____
_____
_____

September 9

Do you consider yourself lucky?

Year _____

_____
_____
_____
_____

Year _____

_____
_____
_____
_____

Year _____

_____
_____
_____
_____

Year _____

_____
_____
_____
_____

Year _____

_____
_____
_____
_____

September 10

What makes you feel insecure?

Year _____

_____
_____
_____
_____

Year _____

_____
_____
_____
_____

Year _____

_____
_____
_____
_____

Year _____

_____
_____
_____
_____

Year _____

_____
_____
_____
_____

September 11

Your definition of an adventure.

Year _____

_____
_____
_____
_____

Year _____

_____
_____
_____
_____

Year _____

_____
_____
_____
_____

Year _____

_____
_____
_____
_____

Year _____

_____
_____
_____
_____

September 12

What's your
go-to comfort food?

Year _____

_____
_____
_____
_____

Year _____

_____
_____
_____
_____

Year _____

_____
_____
_____
_____

Year _____

_____
_____
_____
_____

Year _____

_____
_____
_____
_____

September 13

Favorite city you visited.

Year _____

_____
_____
_____
_____

Year _____

_____
_____
_____
_____

Year _____

_____
_____
_____
_____

Year _____

_____
_____
_____
_____

Year _____

_____
_____
_____
_____

September 14

A luxury you can't live without.

Year _____

_____
_____
_____
_____

Year _____

_____
_____
_____
_____

Year _____

_____
_____
_____
_____

Year _____

_____
_____
_____
_____

Year _____

_____
_____
_____
_____

September 15

What are you grateful for?

Year _____

_____
_____
_____
_____

Year _____

_____
_____
_____
_____

Year _____

_____
_____
_____
_____

Year _____

_____
_____
_____
_____

Year _____

_____
_____
_____
_____

September 16

What are you leaving in the past?

Year _____

_____
_____
_____
_____

Year _____

_____
_____
_____
_____

Year _____

_____
_____
_____
_____

Year _____

_____
_____
_____
_____

Year _____

_____
_____
_____
_____

September 17

What do you forgive yourself for?

Year _____

_____
_____
_____
_____

Year _____

_____
_____
_____
_____

Year _____

_____
_____
_____
_____

Year _____

_____
_____
_____
_____

Year _____

_____
_____
_____
_____

September 18

What are your top priorities?

Year _____

_____
_____
_____
_____

Year _____

_____
_____
_____
_____

Year _____

_____
_____
_____
_____

Year _____

_____
_____
_____
_____

Year _____

_____
_____
_____
_____

September 19

Do you have a bucket list? What
are the top 3 things on it?

Year _____

_____
_____
_____
_____

Year _____

_____
_____
_____
_____

Year _____

_____
_____
_____
_____

Year _____

_____
_____
_____
_____

Year _____

_____
_____
_____
_____

September 20

What's on your mind right now?

Year _____

_____
_____
_____
_____

Year _____

_____
_____
_____
_____

Year _____

_____
_____
_____
_____

Year _____

_____
_____
_____
_____

Year _____

_____
_____
_____
_____

September 21

If you could be anything in the world,
what would you be?

Year _____

_____
_____
_____
_____

Year _____

_____
_____
_____
_____

Year _____

_____
_____
_____
_____

Year _____

_____
_____
_____
_____

Year _____

_____
_____
_____
_____

September 22

How can you love yourself more daily?

Year _____

_____
_____
_____
_____

Year _____

_____
_____
_____
_____

Year _____

_____
_____
_____
_____

Year _____

_____
_____
_____
_____

Year _____

_____
_____
_____
_____

September 23

What are 3 negative mindsets you need to let go of?

Year _____

_____
_____
_____
_____

Year _____

_____
_____
_____
_____

Year _____

_____
_____
_____
_____

Year _____

_____
_____
_____
_____

Year _____

_____
_____
_____
_____

September 24

What areas of your life can you improve and how?

Year _____

_____
_____
_____
_____

Year _____

_____
_____
_____
_____

Year _____

_____
_____
_____
_____

Year _____

_____
_____
_____
_____

Year _____

_____
_____
_____
_____

September 25

Are you doing all that you can to
reach your goals?

Year _____

_____
_____
_____
_____

Year _____

_____
_____
_____
_____

Year _____

_____
_____
_____
_____

Year _____

_____
_____
_____
_____

Year _____

_____
_____
_____

September 26

What makes you upset?

Year _____

_____
_____
_____
_____

Year _____

_____
_____
_____
_____

Year _____

_____
_____
_____
_____

Year _____

_____
_____
_____
_____

Year _____

_____
_____
_____
_____

September 27

Travel by plane or go on a cruise?

Year _____

_____
_____
_____
_____

Year _____

_____
_____
_____
_____

Year _____

_____
_____
_____
_____

Year _____

_____
_____
_____
_____

Year _____

_____
_____
_____
_____

September 28

3 words that define your intentions.

Year _____

_____
_____
_____
_____

Year _____

_____
_____
_____
_____

Year _____

_____
_____
_____
_____

Year _____

_____
_____
_____
_____

Year _____

_____
_____
_____
_____

September 29

When was the last time you
surprised yourself?

Year _____

_____
_____
_____
_____

Year _____

_____
_____
_____
_____

Year _____

_____
_____
_____
_____

Year _____

_____
_____
_____
_____

Year _____

_____
_____
_____
_____

September 30

How important is it to follow trends?

Year _____

_____
_____
_____
_____

Year _____

_____
_____
_____
_____

Year _____

_____
_____
_____
_____

Year _____

_____
_____
_____
_____

Year _____

_____
_____
_____
_____

October 1

What does your schedule for the week look like?

Year _____

_____
_____
_____
_____

Year _____

_____
_____
_____
_____

Year _____

_____
_____
_____
_____

Year _____

_____
_____
_____
_____

Year _____

_____
_____
_____
_____

October 2

Would you like to start a new hobby?

Year _____

_____
_____
_____
_____

Year _____

_____
_____
_____
_____

Year _____

_____
_____
_____
_____

Year _____

_____
_____
_____
_____

Year _____

_____
_____
_____
_____

October 3

Is there someone/something
draining your energy
these days?

Year _____

_____
_____
_____
_____

Year _____

_____
_____
_____
_____

Year _____

_____
_____
_____
_____

Year _____

_____
_____
_____
_____

Year _____

_____
_____
_____
_____

October 4

What's your opinion about meditation?

Year _____

_____
_____
_____
_____

Year _____

_____
_____
_____
_____

Year _____

_____
_____
_____
_____

Year _____

_____
_____
_____
_____

Year _____

_____
_____
_____
_____

October 5

What's your favorite art form?

Year _____

_____
_____
_____
_____

Year _____

_____
_____
_____
_____

Year _____

_____
_____
_____
_____

Year _____

_____
_____
_____
_____

Year _____

_____
_____
_____
_____

October 6

Do you have a bedtime ritual?

Year _____

_____
_____
_____
_____

Year _____

_____
_____
_____
_____

Year _____

_____
_____
_____
_____

Year _____

_____
_____
_____
_____

Year _____

_____
_____
_____
_____

October 7

How many meals do you have per day?

Year _____

_____
_____
_____
_____

Year _____

_____
_____
_____
_____

Year _____

_____
_____
_____
_____

Year _____

_____
_____
_____
_____

Year _____

_____
_____
_____
_____

October 8

Where do you have your meals?

Year _____

_____
_____
_____
_____

Year _____

_____
_____
_____
_____

Year _____

_____
_____
_____
_____

Year _____

_____
_____
_____
_____

Year _____

_____
_____
_____
_____

October 9

How many hours per day do you work?

Year _____

_____
_____
_____
_____

Year _____

_____
_____
_____
_____

Year _____

_____
_____
_____
_____

Year _____

_____
_____
_____
_____

Year _____

_____
_____
_____
_____

October 10

How much are you earning?

Year _____

_____
_____
_____
_____

Year _____

_____
_____
_____
_____

Year _____

_____
_____
_____
_____

Year _____

_____
_____
_____
_____

Year _____

_____
_____
_____
_____

October 11

How do you feel when you
take a break from work?

Year _____

_____
_____
_____
_____

Year _____

_____
_____
_____
_____

Year _____

_____
_____
_____
_____

Year _____

_____
_____
_____
_____

Year _____

_____
_____
_____
_____

October 12

Is there anything you can't live without?

Year _____

_____
_____
_____
_____

Year _____

_____
_____
_____
_____

Year _____

_____
_____
_____
_____

Year _____

_____
_____
_____
_____

Year _____

_____
_____
_____
_____

October 13

How do you describe your time management skills?

Year _____

_____
_____
_____
_____

Year _____

_____
_____
_____
_____

Year _____

_____
_____
_____
_____

Year _____

_____
_____
_____
_____

Year _____

_____
_____
_____
_____

October 14

Do you want/have kids?

Year _____

_____
_____
_____
_____

Year _____

_____
_____
_____
_____

Year _____

_____
_____
_____
_____

Year _____

_____
_____
_____
_____

Year _____

_____
_____
_____
_____

October 15

Favorite season of the year.

Year _____

_____
_____
_____
_____

Year _____

_____
_____
_____
_____

Year _____

_____
_____
_____
_____

Year _____

_____
_____
_____
_____

Year _____

_____
_____
_____
_____

October 16

Mountain or beach?

Year _____

_____
_____
_____
_____

Year _____

_____
_____
_____
_____

Year _____

_____
_____
_____
_____

Year _____

_____
_____
_____
_____

Year _____

_____
_____
_____
_____

October 17

What's your
most important project right now?

Year _____

_____
_____
_____
_____

Year _____

_____
_____
_____
_____

Year _____

_____
_____
_____
_____

Year _____

_____
_____
_____
_____

Year _____

_____
_____
_____
_____

October 18

Would you like to become a volunteer?

Year _____

_____
_____
_____
_____

Year _____

_____
_____
_____
_____

Year _____

_____
_____
_____
_____

Year _____

_____
_____
_____
_____

Year _____

_____
_____
_____
_____

October 19

Your latest thought?

Year _____

_____
_____
_____
_____

Year _____

_____
_____
_____
_____

Year _____

_____
_____
_____
_____

Year _____

_____
_____
_____
_____

Year _____

_____
_____
_____
_____

October 20

How do you take care of your health?

Year _____

_____
_____
_____
_____

Year _____

_____
_____
_____
_____

Year _____

_____
_____
_____
_____

Year _____

_____
_____
_____
_____

Year _____

_____
_____
_____
_____

October 21

Favorite piece of clothing.

Year _____

_____
_____
_____
_____

Year _____

_____
_____
_____
_____

Year _____

_____
_____
_____
_____

Year _____

_____
_____
_____
_____

Year _____

_____
_____
_____
_____

October 22

How many hours did you sleep last night?

Year _____

_____
_____
_____
_____

Year _____

_____
_____
_____
_____

Year _____

_____
_____
_____
_____

Year _____

_____
_____
_____
_____

Year _____

_____
_____
_____
_____

October 23

Silence or background music?

Year _____

_____
_____
_____
_____

Year _____

_____
_____
_____
_____

Year _____

_____
_____
_____
_____

Year _____

_____
_____
_____
_____

Year _____

_____
_____
_____
_____

October 24

What do you wish you had asked your loved ones before they passed away?

Year _____

_____
_____
_____
_____

Year _____

_____
_____
_____
_____

Year _____

_____
_____
_____
_____

Year _____

_____
_____
_____
_____

Year _____

_____
_____
_____
_____

October 25

Is there someone you would like to ask the same question to? Are you still in time?

Year _____

_____
_____
_____
_____

Year _____

_____
_____
_____
_____

Year _____

_____
_____
_____
_____

Year _____

_____
_____
_____
_____

Year _____

_____
_____
_____
_____

October 26

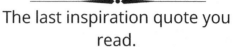

The last inspiration quote you read.

Year _____

_____
_____
_____
_____

Year _____

_____
_____
_____
_____

Year _____

_____
_____
_____
_____

Year _____

_____
_____
_____
_____

Year _____

_____
_____
_____
_____

October 27

What does it mean to you to
make a difference in the world?

Year _____

_____
_____
_____
_____

Year _____

_____
_____
_____
_____

Year _____

_____
_____
_____
_____

Year _____

_____
_____
_____
_____

Year _____

_____
_____
_____
_____

October 28

What would be the best
birthday gift for you?

Year _____

_____
_____
_____
_____

Year _____

_____
_____
_____
_____

Year _____

_____
_____
_____
_____

Year _____

_____
_____
_____
_____

Year _____

_____
_____
_____
_____

October 29

If fear wasn't a problem, what would you do today?

Year _____

_____
_____
_____
_____

Year _____

_____
_____
_____
_____

Year _____

_____
_____
_____
_____

Year _____

_____
_____
_____
_____

Year _____

_____
_____
_____
_____

October 30

What is the best advice you have
received?

Year _____

_____
_____
_____
_____

Year _____

_____
_____
_____
_____

Year _____

_____
_____
_____
_____

Year _____

_____
_____
_____
_____

Year _____

_____
_____
_____
_____

October 31

What is the worst advice you have received?

Year _____

_____
_____
_____
_____

Year _____

_____
_____
_____
_____

Year _____

_____
_____
_____
_____

Year _____

_____
_____
_____
_____

Year _____

_____
_____
_____
_____

November 1

What is one piece of advice you'd give your future self?

Year _____

_____
_____
_____
_____

Year _____

_____
_____
_____
_____

Year _____

_____
_____
_____
_____

Year _____

_____
_____
_____
_____

Year _____

_____
_____
_____
_____

November 2

What will you accomplish next year?

Year _____

_____
_____
_____
_____

Year _____

_____
_____
_____
_____

Year _____

_____
_____
_____
_____

Year _____

_____
_____
_____
_____

Year _____

_____
_____
_____
_____

November 3

How can you show others more love
and compassion each day?

Year _____

_____
_____
_____
_____

Year _____

_____
_____
_____
_____

Year _____

_____
_____
_____
_____

Year _____

_____
_____
_____
_____

Year _____

_____
_____
_____
_____

November 4

What do you think is the most beautiful
thing you've ever seen or experienced?

Year _____

_____
_____
_____
_____

Year _____

_____
_____
_____
_____

Year _____

_____
_____
_____
_____

Year _____

_____
_____
_____
_____

Year _____

_____
_____
_____
_____

November 5

Who makes you the happiest?

Year _____

_____
_____
_____
_____

Year _____

_____
_____
_____
_____

Year _____

_____
_____
_____
_____

Year _____

_____
_____
_____
_____

Year _____

_____
_____
_____
_____

November 6

If you could time travel where would you go?

Year _____

_____
_____
_____
_____

Year _____

_____
_____
_____
_____

Year _____

_____
_____
_____
_____

Year _____

_____
_____
_____
_____

Year _____

_____
_____
_____
_____

November 7

If you could relive one moment what would it be?

Year _____

_____
_____
_____
_____

Year _____

_____
_____
_____
_____

Year _____

_____
_____
_____
_____

Year _____

_____
_____
_____
_____

Year _____

_____
_____
_____
_____

November 8

When was the last time you laughed
until you cried?

Year _____

_____
_____
_____
_____

Year _____

_____
_____
_____
_____

Year _____

_____
_____
_____
_____

Year _____

_____
_____
_____
_____

Year _____

_____
_____
_____
_____

November 9

What is the best gift you have ever received?

Year _____

_____
_____
_____
_____

Year _____

_____
_____
_____
_____

Year _____

_____
_____
_____
_____

Year _____

_____
_____
_____
_____

Year _____

_____
_____
_____
_____

November 10

What do you want to take with you into the future?

Year _____

_____
_____
_____
_____

Year _____

_____
_____
_____
_____

Year _____

_____
_____
_____
_____

Year _____

_____
_____
_____
_____

Year _____

_____
_____
_____
_____

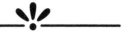

November 11

Can people change?

Year _____

_____
_____
_____
_____

Year _____

_____
_____
_____
_____

Year _____

_____
_____
_____
_____

Year _____

_____
_____
_____
_____

Year _____

_____
_____
_____
_____

November 12

What is your current favorite snack?

Year _____

_____
_____
_____
_____

Year _____

_____
_____
_____
_____

Year _____

_____
_____
_____
_____

Year _____

_____
_____
_____
_____

Year _____

_____
_____
_____
_____

November 13

What is making you mad?

Year _____

_____
_____
_____
_____

Year _____

_____
_____
_____
_____

Year _____

_____
_____
_____
_____

Year _____

_____
_____
_____
_____

Year _____

_____
_____
_____
_____

November 14

How many coffee a day do you drink?

Year _____

_____
_____
_____
_____

Year _____

_____
_____
_____
_____

Year _____

_____
_____
_____
_____

Year _____

_____
_____
_____
_____

Year _____

_____
_____
_____
_____

November 15

What was the hardest thing you're dealing with?

Year _____
_____
_____
_____
_____

Year _____
_____
_____
_____
_____

Year _____
_____
_____
_____
_____

Year _____
_____
_____
_____
_____

Year _____
_____
_____
_____
_____

November 16

Who last called you on the phone?

Year _____

_____
_____
_____
_____

Year _____

_____
_____
_____
_____

Year _____

_____
_____
_____
_____

Year _____

_____
_____
_____
_____

Year _____

_____
_____
_____
_____

November 17

What did you have for dinner today?

Year _____

_____
_____
_____
_____

Year _____

_____
_____
_____
_____

Year _____

_____
_____
_____
_____

Year _____

_____
_____
_____
_____

Year _____

_____
_____
_____
_____

November 18

What are you looking for from life?

Year _____

_____
_____
_____
_____

Year _____

_____
_____
_____
_____

Year _____

_____
_____
_____
_____

Year _____

_____
_____
_____
_____

Year _____

_____
_____
_____
_____

November 19

What is your favorite alchoolic drink?

Year _____

_____
_____
_____
_____

Year _____

_____
_____
_____
_____

Year _____

_____
_____
_____
_____

Year _____

_____
_____
_____
_____

Year _____

_____
_____
_____
_____

November 20

Today I wish I had more ......

Year _____

_____
_____
_____
_____

Year _____

_____
_____
_____
_____

Year _____

_____
_____
_____
_____

Year _____

_____
_____
_____
_____

Year _____

_____
_____
_____
_____

November 21

My house is a home
because ......

Year _____

_____
_____
_____
_____

Year _____

_____
_____
_____
_____

Year _____

_____
_____
_____
_____

Year _____

_____
_____
_____
_____

Year _____

_____
_____
_____
_____

November 22

What's the last thing you apologized for?

Year _____

_____
_____
_____
_____

Year _____

_____
_____
_____
_____

Year _____

_____
_____
_____
_____

Year _____

_____
_____
_____
_____

Year _____

_____
_____
_____
_____

November 23

How many photos did you take today?

Year _____

_____
_____
_____
_____

Year _____

_____
_____
_____
_____

Year _____

_____
_____
_____
_____

Year _____

_____
_____
_____
_____

Year _____

_____
_____
_____
_____

November 24

Last thing you wanted but didn't get.

Year _____

_____
_____
_____
_____

Year _____

_____
_____
_____
_____

Year _____

_____
_____
_____
_____

Year _____

_____
_____
_____
_____

Year _____

_____
_____
_____
_____

November 25

What has challenged your morals?

Year _____

_____
_____
_____
_____

Year _____

_____
_____
_____
_____

Year _____

_____
_____
_____
_____

Year _____

_____
_____
_____
_____

Year _____

_____
_____
_____
_____

November 26

My biggest hope is.....

Year _____

_____
_____
_____
_____

Year _____

_____
_____
_____
_____

Year _____

_____
_____
_____
_____

Year _____

_____
_____
_____
_____

Year _____

_____
_____
_____
_____

November 27

What are three things you need to buy?

Year _____

_____
_____
_____
_____

Year _____

_____
_____
_____
_____

Year _____

_____
_____
_____
_____

Year _____

_____
_____
_____
_____

Year _____

_____
_____
_____
_____

November 28

If money was no object, what would you be doing in your life?

Year _____

_____
_____
_____
_____

Year _____

_____
_____
_____
_____

Year _____

_____
_____
_____
_____

Year _____

_____
_____
_____
_____

Year _____

_____
_____
_____
_____

November 29

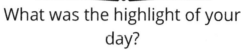

What was the highlight of your day?

Year _____

_____
_____
_____
_____

Year _____

_____
_____
_____
_____

Year _____

_____
_____
_____
_____

Year _____

_____
_____
_____
_____

Year _____

_____
_____
_____
_____

November 30

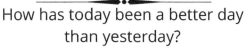

How has today been a better day than yesterday?

Year _____

_____
_____
_____
_____

Year _____

_____
_____
_____
_____

Year _____

_____
_____
_____
_____

Year _____

_____
_____
_____
_____

Year _____

_____
_____
_____
_____

December 1

What is the biggest decision
you've had to make?

Year _____

_____
_____
_____
_____

Year _____

_____
_____
_____
_____

Year _____

_____
_____
_____
_____

Year _____

_____
_____
_____
_____

Year _____

_____
_____
_____
_____

December 2

What has impacted you the most?

Year _____

_____
_____
_____
_____

Year _____

_____
_____
_____
_____

Year _____

_____
_____
_____
_____

Year _____

_____
_____
_____
_____

Year _____

_____
_____
_____
_____

December 3

What have you learned during the pandemic?

Year _____

_____
_____
_____
_____

Year _____

_____
_____
_____
_____

Year _____

_____
_____
_____
_____

Year _____

_____
_____
_____
_____

Year _____

_____
_____
_____
_____

December 4

How do you help others?

Year _____

_____
_____
_____
_____

Year _____

_____
_____
_____
_____

Year _____

_____
_____
_____
_____

Year _____

_____
_____
_____
_____

Year _____

_____
_____
_____
_____

December 5

How do you like to spend your weekends?

Year _____

_____
_____
_____
_____

Year _____

_____
_____
_____
_____

Year _____

_____
_____
_____
_____

Year _____

_____
_____
_____
_____

Year _____

_____
_____
_____
_____

December 6

Do you prefer going out or
staying in?

Year _____

_____
_____
_____
_____

Year _____

_____
_____
_____
_____

Year _____

_____
_____
_____
_____

Year _____

_____
_____
_____
_____

Year _____

_____
_____
_____
_____

December 7

If you could have any superpower, what would it be?

Year _____

_____
_____
_____
_____

Year _____

_____
_____
_____
_____

Year _____

_____
_____
_____
_____

Year _____

_____
_____
_____
_____

Year _____

_____
_____
_____
_____

December 8

Are you currently pushing yourself to your fullest potential?

Year _____

_____
_____
_____
_____

Year _____

_____
_____
_____
_____

Year _____

_____
_____
_____
_____

Year _____

_____
_____
_____
_____

Year _____

_____
_____
_____
_____

December 9

What will you accomplish before
the end of the year?

Year _____

_____
_____
_____
_____

Year _____

_____
_____
_____
_____

Year _____

_____
_____
_____
_____

Year _____

_____
_____
_____
_____

Year _____

_____
_____
_____
_____

December 10

Your last DIY project?

Year _____

_____
_____
_____
_____

Year _____

_____
_____
_____
_____

Year _____

_____
_____
_____
_____

Year _____

_____
_____
_____
_____

Year _____

_____
_____
_____
_____

December 11

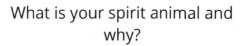

What is your spirit animal and why?

Year _____

_____
_____
_____
_____

Year _____

_____
_____
_____
_____

Year _____

_____
_____
_____
_____

Year _____

_____
_____
_____
_____

Year _____

_____
_____
_____
_____

December 12

Happy/positive news you recently heard.

Year _____

_____
_____
_____
_____

Year _____

_____
_____
_____
_____

Year _____

_____
_____
_____
_____

Year _____

_____
_____
_____
_____

Year _____

_____
_____
_____
_____

December 13

Describe happiness.

Year _____

_____
_____
_____
_____

Year _____

_____
_____
_____
_____

Year _____

_____
_____
_____
_____

Year _____

_____
_____
_____
_____

Year _____

_____
_____
_____
_____

December 14

What do you do to stay focused?

Year _____

_____
_____
_____
_____

Year _____

_____
_____
_____
_____

Year _____

_____
_____
_____
_____

Year _____

_____
_____
_____
_____

Year _____

_____
_____
_____
_____

December 15

What was the most important event of today?

Year _____

_____
_____
_____
_____

Year _____

_____
_____
_____
_____

Year _____

_____
_____
_____
_____

Year _____

_____
_____
_____
_____

Year _____

_____
_____
_____
_____

December 16

What's your favorite dish?

Year _____

_____
_____
_____
_____

Year _____

_____
_____
_____
_____

Year _____

_____
_____
_____
_____

Year _____

_____
_____
_____
_____

Year _____

_____
_____
_____
_____

December 17

First thought when you woke up today (that you remember).

Year _____

_____
_____
_____
_____

Year _____

_____
_____
_____
_____

Year _____

_____
_____
_____
_____

Year _____

_____
_____
_____
_____

Year _____

_____
_____
_____
_____

December 18

What was your biggest victory yesterday?

Year _____

_____
_____
_____
_____

Year _____

_____
_____
_____
_____

Year _____

_____
_____
_____
_____

Year _____

_____
_____
_____
_____

Year _____

_____
_____
_____
_____

December 19

What's your favorite TV show at the moment?

Year _____

_____
_____
_____
_____

Year _____

_____
_____
_____
_____

Year _____

_____
_____
_____
_____

Year _____

_____
_____
_____
_____

Year _____

_____
_____
_____
_____

December 20

Where would you like to be right now?

Year _____

_____
_____
_____
_____

Year _____

_____
_____
_____
_____

Year _____

_____
_____
_____
_____

Year _____

_____
_____
_____
_____

Year _____

_____
_____
_____
_____

December 21

What's your (favorite) hobby?

Year _____

_____
_____
_____
_____

Year _____

_____
_____
_____
_____

Year _____

_____
_____
_____
_____

Year _____

_____
_____
_____
_____

Year _____

_____
_____
_____
_____

December 22

What do you do when life gets hard?

Year _____
_____
_____
_____
_____

Year _____
_____
_____
_____
_____

Year _____
_____
_____
_____
_____

Year _____
_____
_____
_____
_____

Year _____
_____
_____
_____
_____

December 23

If you could make 1 wish come true, what would it be?

Year _____

_____
_____
_____
_____

Year _____

_____
_____
_____
_____

Year _____

_____
_____
_____
_____

Year _____

_____
_____
_____
_____

Year _____

_____
_____
_____
_____

December 24

What brought you joy today?

Year _____

_____
_____
_____
_____

Year _____

_____
_____
_____
_____

Year _____

_____
_____
_____
_____

Year _____

_____
_____
_____
_____

Year _____

_____
_____
_____
_____

December 25

What do you wish for this Christmas?

Year _____

_____
_____
_____
_____

Year _____

_____
_____
_____
_____

Year _____

_____
_____
_____
_____

Year _____

_____
_____
_____
_____

Year _____

_____
_____
_____
_____

December 26

What's your Purpose in life?

Year _____

_____
_____
_____
_____

Year _____

_____
_____
_____
_____

Year _____

_____
_____
_____
_____

Year _____

_____
_____
_____
_____

Year _____

_____
_____
_____
_____

December 27

What causes you anxiety?

Year _____

_____
_____
_____
_____

Year _____

_____
_____
_____
_____

Year _____

_____
_____
_____
_____

Year _____

_____
_____
_____
_____

Year _____

_____
_____
_____
_____

December 28

Do you procrastinate on a regular basis?

Year _____

_____
_____
_____
_____

Year _____

_____
_____
_____
_____

Year _____

_____
_____
_____
_____

Year _____

_____
_____
_____
_____

Year _____

_____
_____
_____
_____

December 29
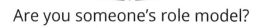

Are you someone's role model?

Year _____

_____
_____
_____
_____

Year _____

_____
_____
_____
_____

Year _____

_____
_____
_____
_____

Year _____

_____
_____
_____
_____

Year _____

_____
_____
_____
_____

December 30

What is your new year resolution?

Year _____

_____
_____
_____
_____

Year _____

_____
_____
_____
_____

Year _____

_____
_____
_____
_____

Year _____

_____
_____
_____
_____

Year _____

_____
_____
_____
_____

December 31

Describe the past month in
one word.

Year _____

_____
_____
_____
_____

Year _____

_____
_____
_____
_____

Year _____

_____
_____
_____
_____

Year _____

_____
_____
_____
_____

Year _____

_____
_____
_____
_____